paperblanks®
TRIBAL EMBROIDERY

Die traditionellen Stickereien aus der Region Kutsch im indischen Bundesstaat Gujarat sind berühmt für ihre fantasievollen Muster auf farbenprächtigem Patchwork-Untergrund. Die mit Pflanzenfarben eingefärbten Stoffe werden mit bunten Baumwollfäden und glitzernden Metallfäden bestickt und mit Metall- oder Spiegelstückchen, Perlen und kleinen Muscheln verziert. Dieses Notizbuch, das die leuchtenden Farben und wundervollen Designs dieser außergewöhnlichen Kunst genau wiedergibt, ist den traditionellen Stickereien Indiens gewidmet.

I tessuti ricamati tribali della regione Kutch, India sono rinomati per i loro magici patchwork di stoffa colorata con tinture vegetali e riccamente decorata con luccicanti paillette metalliche o specchietti, perline e piccole conchiglie cucite con filo metallico ricamato a catenella. Questo libro, che riproduce la luminosità di questa forma d'arte impressionante, è dedicata alla tradizione Indiana del ricamo tribale.

La broderie tribale de la région du Kutch (Gujarat, Inde) est célèbre pour ses éblouissants motifs sur fond de patchwork en tissus végétal coloré et tissé de paillettes, perles et petits coquillages scintillants par divers fils en coton coloré et du fil métallique au point de chaînette chatoyant. Imprimé de façon à reproduire exactement la luminosité et l'aspect de cet art saisissant, ce journal est un hommage à la tradition indienne de la broderie tribale.

Los bordados tribales de Kutch, en el estado indio de Gujarat, son populares por sus extraordinarios diseños, que decoran un mosaico de colores mágicos sobre tejidos tratados con tintes vegetales. Brillantes lentejuelas metálicas y plateadas, abalorios y pequeñas conchas adornan estos tejidos, cosidos con hilo de algodón de varios colores e hilo metálico brillante en cadeneta. Este diario, que recrea la luminosidad y ornamentación de esta vistosa forma de arte, está dedicado a la tradición de los bordados tribales de la India.

世にも名高い、インドのグジャラート州カチ地方の民族刺繍。天然の色素で染め上げた、そもいわれぬ風合いの布をはぎ合わせた上に、目くるめくようなデザインを施しています。きらきらと光るスパンコールやビーズ、そして小さな貝殻を配し、様々な色の木綿糸やメタリックな糸でチェーンスティッチを入れた、驚くべき芸術品。本ノートブックはその輝きと質感をそのままに再現した、インドの刺繍文化への讃歌です。

TRIBAL EMBROIDERY

Sequined Garnet

Tribal embroidery from the Kutch area of Gujarat in India is renowned for its stunning designs patterned on a magically coloured patchwork background of vegetable-dyed fabric. Brilliant metallic or mirror sequins, beads, and small shells are embroidered onto this fabric with varying colours of cotton thread and sparkling chain-stitched metallic thread. Exactingly printed to recreate the luminosity and look of this striking art form, this journal is dedicated to the tribal embroidery tradition of India.

ISBN-10: 1-55156-760-1   ISBN-13: 978-1-55156-760-0
SLIM FORMAT   176 PAGES   LINED

Printed on acid-free sustainable forest paper.
© 2001, 2007 Hartley & Marks Publishers Inc. All rights reserved.
No part of this book may be reproduced without written permission from the publisher. Paperblanks® are published by
Hartley & Marks Publishers Inc. Made in China.
North America 1-800-277-5887
Europe +800-3333-8005
Japan 0120-177-153

www.paperblanks.com